P9-CCP-601

DREAM BIG!

Proudly donated by **Bank of America**

The editors would like to thank
BARBARA KIEFER, Ph.D.,
Charlotte S. Huck Professor of Children's Literature,
The Ohio State University, and
LANE J. BRUNNER, R.Ph., Ph.D.,
Dean, School of Pharmacy,
Regis University,
for their assistance in the preparation of this book.

Visit us on the Web!
www.randomhouse.com/kids
Seussville.com

Educators and librarians, for a variety of teaching tools, visit us at
www.randomhouse.com/teachers

Library of Congress Cataloging-in-Publication Data
Worth, Bonnie.
One cent, two cents, old cent, new cent : all about money / by Bonnie Worth ; illustrated by
Aristides Ruiz and Joe Mathieu.
    p. cm.
Includes index.
ISBN 978-0-375-82881-2 (trade) — ISBN 978-0-375-92881-9 (lib. bdg.)
1. Money—Juvenile literature. 2. Arithmetic—Juvenile literature. I. Ruiz, Aristides.
II. Mathieu, Joseph. III. Title.
HG221.5.W67 2008 332.4—dc22 2007003790

Printed in the United States of America
19 18 17

One Cent, Two Cents, Old Cent, New Cent

by Bonnie Worth

illustrated by Aristides Ruiz and Joe Mathieu

The Cat in the Hat's Learning Library®

Random House 🏠 New York

I'm the Cat in the Hat
and you know something funny?
We're about to have fun
learning all about money!

Where does it come from?
Can you answer that, please?
I will give you a hint:
It does not grow on trees!

MUSEUM
of
MONEY

MYTHICAL MONEY TREE

Just one penny each
it will cost you to see
the Museum of Money.
Step up and pay me!

People bartered to buy things
in ancient times.
They did not have pennies,
or nickels, or dimes.

This meant that a beekeeper
might want to swap
his store of honey
for a farmer's wheat crop.

BARTERING

If the farmer liked honey,
a deal could be struck.
If the farmer liked jam,
it was the keeper's bad luck.

People would fight
over deals that they made.
Was this a good swap?
Did I make a fair trade?

Perhaps that is why
money was invented.
It was easier to use
and decay was prevented.

It was easy to carry
and count, and what's more,
it was easy to save
and was easy to store.

What's an old form of money?
I'm so glad you asked me.
I'll give you a hint:
it came from the sea.

Seashells were used
to barter and trade.
A handful of shells
and you had it made!

Feathers and eggs
and leather and jade
are some other things
from which money was made.

But eggs could get scrambled
and leather got dirty.

Money needed to last
and be solid and sturdy.

So people mined ore—
copper, silver, and gold.

They melted it down,
poured it into a mold.

In the shape of a bar
these ingots were made.

Folks hauled them around
and would use them in trade.

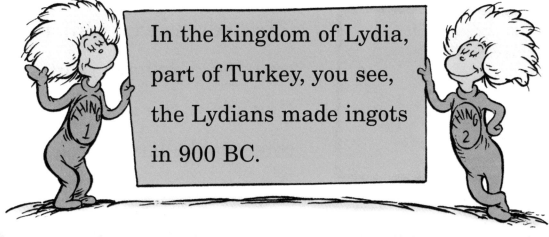

In the kingdom of Lydia,
part of Turkey, you see,
the Lydians made ingots
in 900 BC.

Then someone in Lydia
had a brainstorm:
Make metal coins!
(A far handier form!)

We've dug up these coins
all over the place.
Each coin has a lion's head
stamped on its face.

The Lydians were sailors,
and you may have read
that's how the use of their
coins might have spread.

Here is a fact I am
happy to tell you:
Folks other places
began to make coins, too.

In China, the farthest
of Far Eastern places,
some coins shaped like cowries
had lines on their faces.

Other coins contained holes
for a string to pass through.
So coins could be carried
together with you.

A string of such coins
added up to a cache.
You tied up the string
on a belt or a sash.

In Greece, they stamped coins
with various things,
like a picture of Pegasus,
the horse who had wings.

This coin has an owl
on its face, and my guess
is it stood for Athena,
the wisest goddess.

Now even today
some heads of state
put their heads onto coins
like Caesar the great.

Here is a fact that we
think is so neat.
Money's made in a mint.
(Not the kind that you eat!)

Thing One and Thing Two
are about to mint dimes.
Mints work much the same
as in ancient times.

How to Make a Dime
One Step at a Time!

(This is brought to you
by Thing One and Thing Two!)

1. Heat metals together until they are hot and melted to goop inside of a pot.

2. Pour goop in a cast, also known as a mold.

3. Strike goop with an image before it turns cold.

4. Remove from the cast. (Oh, isn't this funny?) Time to have fun with your shiny new money!

Ancients kept money where
they prayed and gave thanks.
In this way the temples
became the first banks.

To temple you went
to save or to borrow
for as long as two years
or as short as tomorrow.

Interest is the name
for the fee that you owe
to the bank for the money
they loan you, you know.

When your money is saved
in a savings account,
the bank then pays you
a smallish amount.

This smallish amount
that the bank pays to you
is the interest you've earned,
and it's only your due.

The smallest coin ever
is so hard to see!
(See the Indian fanam
next to that BB?)

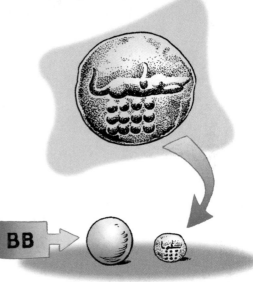

BB →

You would think that they might
lose count of their hoard,
but dents in some wood
make a neat counting board.

From the islands of Yap
come the heaviest ones:
Limestone coins eight feet wide,
each weighing three tons!

Carrying these coins,
some Yap ships sank.
Could you fit a Yap coin
in *your* piggy bank?

Traveling to parts
of the New World with me,
here are some Spanish coins
I would like you to see.

Spain's explorers sent home
from the New World as freight
golden doubloons
and pieces of eight.

The most valuable coins
in those parts were these.
To steal them, some pirates
sailed all seven seas.

American settlers
minted coins such as these,
stamped with the image
of local trees.

For money, the natives
strung seashells and beads
into belts of wampum
for their trading needs.

When it became
a new nation and free,
the United States minted
its own currency.

I have some with me
(as you see, I have many).
The kind that I have is
the little red penny.

It was made in the year
seventeen ninety-three.
Here's one that's a half-cent
you might like to see!

Here is another one.

It's also red.

It's the penny we know

as the Indian Head.

In nineteen oh nine (that's the year
I am thinkin'),
we began to mint pennies
with the face of Abe Lincoln.

During World War Two
(a brave time, I do feel),
pennies were made
out of zinc-coated steel.

We needed the copper
for wartime, but then
after the war
we used copper again.

Some pennies I've shown you
from so long ago
are worth nearly
one thousand dollars or so!

Here is a great word
you can add to your list:
A collector of coins
is a numismatist!

Pennies to dollars . . .
we mint the whole range.
But mostly we use all
these coins to make change.

It's paper that's king,
but paper gets rotten,
so we make paper money
from linen and cotton.

When you study your money
(and these days, who bothers?),
you will find on it faces
of our nation's fathers.

GEORGE WASHINGTON

THOMAS JEFFERSON

What's the dollar sign mean?
Could it be? Take a guess!
Does it come from a U
printed under an S?

My numismatist friend
has told me of late
it might come from the
Spanish pieces of eight.

BENJAMIN
FRANKLIN

ANDREW
JACKSON

ULYSSES S.
GRANT

ABRAHAM LINCOLN

ALEXANDER HAMILTON

On the ten thousand bill
you will find the face
of Abe Lincoln's treasurer,
Salmon Portland Chase!

Will you find one around?
No, you probably won't.
They no longer print bills
of this size. No, they don't.

If they print them again,
do you think maybe that
they might use the face of . . .

40

GLOSSARY

Ancient: Of a time long in the past.

BB: A teeny-tiny metal ball made to be shot from a gun.

Copper: A metal that is mined from the earth and is soft and easy to bend.

Cowrie: An egg-shaped shell that is usually smooth and shiny on one side, with a long, narrow opening across the other.

Doubloon: A gold coin used by the Spanish centuries ago.

Jade: A greenish stone used for carving.

Limestone: A kind of stone often used for building and used to make lime, which is one ingredient of cement.

Steel: A manufactured metal made of different kinds of iron and known for its hardness and strength.

Temple: A special building where people go to worship their god or gods.

Treasurer: Someone responsible for receiving, keeping, and distributing money.

Zinc: A bluish white metal that is mined from the earth and used to coat other kinds of metal.

FOR FURTHER READING

The Berenstain Bears' Trouble with Money by Stan and Jan Berenstain (Random House, *First Time Books*). Brother and Sister Bear learn about spending money wisely. For ages 5–8.

A Dollar for Penny by Dr. Julie Glass, illustrated by Joy Allen (Random House, *Step into Reading*). A young girl learns about counting coins and earning money when she opens a lemonade stand. For ages 4–6.

Follow the Money! by Loreen Leedy (Holiday House). Follow a brand-new quarter on all the stops "he" makes after leaving the mint. For kindergarten and up.

Money by Joe Cribb and Laura Buller (Dorling Kindersley, *Eyewitness Books*). Amazing photographs show many different types of money and demonstrate how it's made. For ages 8 and up.

Smart About Money: A Rich History by Jon Anderson, illustrated by Thor Wickstrom (Grosset & Dunlap, *Smart About History*). A young boy who loves money decides to research it for a school report. For ages 4–8.

The Story of Money by Betsy Maestro, illustrated by Giulio Maestro (HarperTrophy). All about the history of money. For ages 7 and up.

INDEX